EMMANUEL JOSEPH

Bold Strokes, Gentle Hands, Creativity, Self-Compassion, and the Art of Building Together

Copyright © 2025 by Emmanuel Joseph

All rights reserved. No part of this publication may be reproduced, stored or transmitted in any form or by any means, electronic, mechanical, photocopying, recording, scanning, or otherwise without written permission from the publisher. It is illegal to copy this book, post it to a website, or distribute it by any other means without permission.

First edition

This book was professionally typeset on Reedsy.
Find out more at reedsy.com

Contents

1. Chapter 1: Embracing the Blank Canvas — 1
2. Chapter 2: The Dance of Ideas — 3
3. Chapter 3: The Power of Play — 5
4. Chapter 4: The Art of Reflection — 7
5. Chapter 5: Overcoming Creative Blocks — 9
6. Chapter 6: Finding Inspiration in Everyday Life — 11
7. Chapter 7: The Healing Power of Creativity — 13
8. Chapter 8: The Balance of Structure and Freedom — 15
9. Chapter 9: The Magic of Flow — 17
10. Chapter 10: The Art of Perseverance — 18
11. Chapter 11: The Joy of Experimentation — 19
12. Chapter 12: The Beauty of Imperfection — 21
13. Chapter 13: The Spirit of Collaboration — 23
14. Chapter 14: The Gift of Gratitude — 25
15. Chapter 15: The Legacy of Creativity — 27
16. Chapter 16: The Journey of Self-Discovery — 29
17. Chapter 17: The Art of Building Together — 31

1

Chapter 1: Embracing the Blank Canvas

In the heart of every creative endeavor lies an empty space yearning to be filled. The blank canvas, whether it be a literal piece of cloth stretched on a frame, a blank page in a journal, or an unformed idea in the mind, invites the creator to unleash their imagination. The fear of making that first mark can be paralyzing, yet it is in overcoming this fear that the journey begins. To embark on this journey, one must understand that creativity is not about perfection but about exploration and expression.

As we approach the blank canvas, self-compassion becomes our guiding light. It is easy to criticize ourselves before we even begin, but by embracing a kind and gentle attitude towards our own efforts, we can free ourselves from the chains of self-doubt. By viewing mistakes as opportunities for growth rather than failures, we cultivate an environment where creativity can thrive. The act of creating becomes an act of self-love, nurturing our spirit and fostering a sense of accomplishment.

The process of building together with others adds another layer of richness to our creative endeavors. Collaboration allows us to merge diverse perspectives and skills, resulting in creations that are greater than the sum of their parts. It is through the shared experience of co-creation that we learn the value of empathy, communication, and mutual respect. In this space, we celebrate each other's unique contributions and find joy in the collective process.

Ultimately, the blank canvas is not something to be feared, but a space of infinite possibility. It is a reminder that within each of us lies the potential to create, to express, and to connect. By embracing this potential with bold strokes and gentle hands, we open ourselves to a world of creativity and compassion.

2

Chapter 2: The Dance of Ideas

Ideas often arrive unannounced, like unexpected guests at a party. They swirl around in our minds, colliding and intertwining, until one stands out and demands attention. The dance of ideas is a dynamic and fluid process, where creativity flows freely and inspiration strikes at the most unexpected moments. This dance is a testament to the boundless nature of the human mind, capable of generating an endless stream of possibilities.

In this dance, self-compassion plays a crucial role. It is easy to dismiss our ideas as trivial or unworthy, but by treating each idea with kindness and curiosity, we allow them to flourish. Self-compassion encourages us to take risks, to explore new avenues, and to embrace the unknown. It is through this gentle approach that we create a fertile ground for innovation and discovery.

Building together with others enhances the dance of ideas, as collaboration sparks new insights and perspectives. When we share our thoughts and brainstorm with others, we create a symphony of creativity that resonates with depth and complexity. The exchange of ideas fosters a sense of community and collective growth, where each contribution is valued and celebrated. In this collaborative dance, we learn the importance of active listening, open-mindedness, and the willingness to adapt.

The dance of ideas is a continuous and evolving journey. It is a celebration of the creative spirit that resides within each of us, and a testament to the power of imagination. By approaching this dance with bold strokes and gentle hands, we honor our own creativity and the creativity of those around us.

3

Chapter 3: The Power of Play

Play is a powerful and often overlooked aspect of creativity. It is through play that we tap into our most authentic selves, shedding the constraints of societal expectations and allowing our imagination to run wild. The act of play is a joyful and liberating experience, where we experiment, take risks, and discover new possibilities. It is in this state of play that our creativity flourishes and our ideas take flight.

Self-compassion is essential in embracing the power of play. It encourages us to let go of our fear of judgment and to approach our creative endeavors with a sense of curiosity and wonder. By being kind to ourselves and embracing our playful side, we create a safe space where we can explore and express freely. Self-compassion allows us to find joy in the process of creation, rather than focusing solely on the end result.

Building together through play fosters a sense of connection and camaraderie. When we engage in playful activities with others, we build trust, strengthen relationships, and create a sense of shared purpose. Playful collaboration encourages us to think outside the box, to challenge each other's ideas, and to find innovative solutions. In this playful environment, we celebrate each other's creativity and find joy in the collective experience.

The power of play is a reminder that creativity is not a rigid and structured process, but a dynamic and evolving journey. It is through play that we tap into our true creative potential and find inspiration in the most unexpected places. By embracing the power of play with bold strokes and gentle hands, we unlock a world of creativity and self-compassion.

4

Chapter 4: The Art of Reflection

Reflection is a vital component of the creative process, allowing us to pause, assess, and gain insights from our experiences. It is through reflection that we deepen our understanding of our creative journey, identify areas for growth, and celebrate our accomplishments. The art of reflection is a practice of self-awareness and mindfulness, where we take the time to appreciate the beauty of our creations and the lessons they teach us.

Self-compassion is integral to the art of reflection, as it encourages us to approach our reflections with kindness and non-judgment. By being gentle with ourselves, we create a space where we can acknowledge our achievements and learn from our mistakes without harsh criticism. Self-compassion allows us to embrace our imperfections and see them as opportunities for growth and self-improvement.

Building together through reflection enhances our collective creativity and fosters a sense of shared growth. When we reflect with others, we gain diverse perspectives and insights that enrich our understanding of our creative process. Collaborative reflection encourages open and honest communication, where we can share our successes, challenges, and aspirations. In this reflective space, we support each other's growth and celebrate our collective achievements.

The art of reflection is a continuous and evolving practice. It is a reminder that creativity is not just about producing tangible results, but about the journey of self-discovery and growth. By embracing the art of reflection with bold strokes and gentle hands, we deepen our connection to our creativity and cultivate a sense of self-compassion and collective growth.

5

Chapter 5: Overcoming Creative Blocks

Creative blocks are an inevitable part of the creative journey, but they do not have to be a source of frustration and despair. Instead, they can be seen as opportunities for growth and exploration. Overcoming creative blocks requires a combination of perseverance, self-compassion, and a willingness to explore new approaches. It is through this process that we learn to navigate challenges and find new avenues for creative expression.

Self-compassion is crucial in overcoming creative blocks, as it encourages us to be gentle with ourselves during times of struggle. By acknowledging our feelings of frustration and self-doubt, we create a space where we can address our challenges with kindness and understanding. Self-compassion allows us to take breaks, seek support, and approach our creative blocks with a sense of curiosity rather than judgment.

Building together with others can be a powerful tool in overcoming creative blocks. Collaboration provides fresh perspectives, new ideas, and a sense of accountability. When we share our struggles with others, we gain support and encouragement that can help us navigate our creative blocks. Collaborative problem-solving fosters a sense of community and mutual growth, where we learn from each other's experiences and find innovative solutions.

Overcoming creative blocks is a testament to the resilience and determination of the creative spirit. It is a reminder that creativity is not a linear process, but a journey filled with peaks and valleys. By embracing this journey with bold strokes and gentle hands, we cultivate a sense of self-compassion and resilience that allows us to overcome obstacles and continue to create.

6

Chapter 6: Finding Inspiration in Everyday Life

Inspiration can be found in the most unexpected places, often hidden in the ordinary moments of our daily lives. By cultivating a sense of mindfulness and curiosity, we can discover beauty and creativity in the world around us. Finding inspiration in everyday life is about being present, open, and receptive to the wonders of the world.

Self-compassion plays a key role in finding inspiration, as it encourages us to slow down and appreciate the present moment. By being kind to ourselves and taking the time to savor our experiences, we create a space where inspiration can flow freely. Self-compassion allows us to see the beauty in the ordinary and find joy in the simple pleasures of life.

Building together with others enhances our ability to find inspiration, as collaboration opens our eyes to new perspectives and experiences. When we share our discoveries with others, we create a sense of connection and collective inspiration. Collaborative exploration fosters a sense of curiosity and wonder, where we learn from each other's insights and find new ways to appreciate the world around us.

Finding inspiration in everyday life is a practice of mindfulness and gratitude. It is a reminder that creativity is not confined to grand gestures and monumental achievements, but can be found in the small moments that make up our daily lives. By embracing this practice with bold strokes and gentle hands, we cultivate a sense of self-compassion and a deep appreciation for the world around us.

7

Chapter 7: The Healing Power of Creativity

Creativity has the power to heal, transforming our pain and struggles into expressions of hope and resilience. Through creative endeavors, we can process our emotions, find solace, and create meaning from our experiences. The healing power of creativity lies in its ability to connect us to our inner selves and provide a sense of purpose and fulfillment.

Self-compassion is essential in harnessing the healing power of creativity, as it encourages us to approach our creative endeavors with a sense of gentleness and understanding. By being kind to ourselves and acknowledging our emotions, we create a space where healing can occur. Self-compassion allows us to express our pain and struggles through creative outlets, turning them into symbols of strength and resilience.

Building together with others enhances the healing power of creativity, as collaboration provides support, empathy, and a sense of community. When we create together, we share our stories and experiences, fostering a sense of connection and understanding. Collaborative creativity encourages us to find strength in our collective experiences and to heal through shared expression.

The healing power of creativity is a testament to the transformative nature of the creative process. It is a reminder that our creativity can be a source of solace and strength, helping us navigate life's challenges and find meaning in our experiences. By embracing this healing power with bold strokes and gentle hands, we cultivate a sense of self-compassion and resilience that allows us to create and heal.

8

Chapter 8: The Balance of Structure and Freedom

Creativity thrives in an environment where structure and freedom coexist. Structure provides a framework that guides our creative efforts, while freedom allows us to explore and experiment within that framework. Finding the balance between structure and freedom is essential in nurturing our creativity and fostering a sense of self-compassion.

Self-compassion plays a key role in achieving this balance, as it encourages us to be kind to ourselves and to trust the creative process. By being gentle with ourselves and acknowledging our need for both structure and freedom, we create a space where creativity can flourish. Self-compassion allows us to set boundaries while also embracing the spontaneity and unpredictability of the creative journey.

Building together with others enhances our ability to find this balance, as collaboration provides diverse perspectives and insights. When we create together, we learn from each other's approaches and find new ways to integrate structure and freedom into our creative process. Collaborative creativity fosters a sense of mutual support and growth, where we celebrate each other's contributions and find joy in the collective experience.

The balance of structure and freedom is a reminder that creativity is not a rigid or chaotic process, but a harmonious interplay of guidance and exploration. By embracing this balance with bold strokes and gentle hands, we cultivate a sense of self-compassion and creativity that allows us to create and connect.

9

Chapter 9: The Magic of Flow

Flow is a state of being where creativity flows effortlessly and time seems to stand still. It is in this state that we are fully immersed in our creative endeavors, experiencing a sense of joy and fulfillment. The magic of flow lies in its ability to connect us to our true selves and to the present moment, allowing our creativity to shine.

Self-compassion is essential in achieving flow, as it encourages us to be kind to ourselves and to embrace the creative process. By being gentle with ourselves and acknowledging our need for focus and immersion, we create a space where flow can occur. Self-compassion allows us to let go of distractions and to fully engage in our creative activities.

Building together with others enhances our ability to achieve flow, as collaboration provides support and encouragement. When we create together, we share our energy and enthusiasm, fostering a sense of collective flow. Collaborative creativity encourages us to find joy in the shared experience and to celebrate each other's contributions.

The magic of flow is a reminder that creativity is not just about producing tangible results, but about experiencing the joy and fulfillment of the creative process. By embracing this magic with bold strokes and gentle hands, we cultivate a sense of self-compassion and creativity that allows us to create and connect.

10

Chapter 10: The Art of Perseverance

Perseverance is a vital component of the creative journey, allowing us to overcome challenges and continue creating despite setbacks. The art of perseverance is a practice of resilience and determination, where we push through obstacles and find new ways to express our creativity.

Self-compassion plays a crucial role in the art of perseverance, as it encourages us to be kind to ourselves during times of struggle. By acknowledging our feelings of frustration and self-doubt, we create a space where we can address our challenges with kindness and understanding. Self-compassion allows us to take breaks, seek support, and approach our creative blocks with a sense of curiosity rather than judgment.

Building together with others can be a powerful tool in the art of perseverance. Collaboration provides fresh perspectives, new ideas, and a sense of accountability. When we share our struggles with others, we gain support and encouragement that can help us navigate our creative blocks. Collaborative problem-solving fosters a sense of community and mutual growth, where we learn from each other's experiences and find innovative solutions.

The art of perseverance is a testament to the resilience and determination of the creative spirit. It is a reminder that creativity is not a linear process, but a journey filled with peaks and valleys. By embracing this journey with bold strokes and gentle hands, we cultivate a sense of self-compassion and resilience that allows us to overcome obstacles and continue to create.

11

Chapter 11: The Joy of Experimentation

Experimentation is a joyful and liberating aspect of creativity, allowing us to explore new ideas and techniques without fear of failure. The joy of experimentation lies in its ability to foster a sense of curiosity and wonder, where we can discover new possibilities and push the boundaries of our creativity.

Self-compassion is essential in embracing the joy of experimentation, as it encourages us to be kind to ourselves and to approach our creative endeavors with a sense of curiosity and wonder. By being gentle with ourselves and acknowledging our need for exploration, we create a space where experimentation can occur. Self-compassion allows us to find joy in the process of creation, rather than focusing solely on the end result.

Building together through experimentation enhances our creative journey, as collaboration provides fresh perspectives and new ideas. When we experiment together, we share our discoveries and insights, fostering a sense of collective curiosity and growth. Collaborative experimentation encourages us to think outside the box, to challenge each other's ideas, and to find innovative solutions.

The joy of experimentation is a reminder that creativity is not a rigid and structured process, but a dynamic and evolving journey. It is through experimentation that we tap into our true creative potential and find inspiration in the most unexpected places. By embracing the joy of experimentation with bold strokes and gentle hands, we unlock a world of creativity and self-compassion.

12

Chapter 12: The Beauty of Imperfection

Imperfection is a natural and inherent part of the creative process, and it is through embracing imperfection that we find beauty and authenticity in our creations. The beauty of imperfection lies in its ability to connect us to our true selves and to the world around us, allowing us to express our creativity with honesty and vulnerability.

Self-compassion is crucial in embracing the beauty of imperfection, as it encourages us to be kind to ourselves and to view our imperfections as opportunities for growth. By being gentle with ourselves and acknowledging our need for authenticity, we create a space where imperfection can be celebrated. Self-compassion allows us to let go of the pursuit of perfection and to find joy in the process of creation.

Building together with others enhances our ability to embrace imperfection, as collaboration provides support and encouragement. When we create together, we share our stories and experiences, fostering a sense of connection and understanding. Collaborative creativity encourages us to find strength in our collective imperfections and to heal through shared expression.

The beauty of imperfection is a testament to the transformative nature of the creative process. It is a reminder that our creativity can be a source of solace and strength, helping us navigate life's challenges and find meaning in our experiences. By embracing this beauty with bold strokes and gentle hands, we cultivate a sense of self-compassion and resilience that allows us to create and heal.

13

Chapter 13: The Spirit of Collaboration

Collaboration is a powerful and enriching aspect of the creative process, allowing us to merge diverse perspectives and skills to create something greater than the sum of its parts. The spirit of collaboration lies in its ability to foster a sense of connection and collective growth, where we celebrate each other's unique contributions and find joy in the shared experience.

Self-compassion plays a key role in nurturing the spirit of collaboration, as it encourages us to approach our collaborative efforts with kindness and respect. By being gentle with ourselves and acknowledging our need for mutual support, we create a space where collaboration can thrive. Self-compassion allows us to communicate openly, to listen actively, and to embrace the contributions of others.

Building together through collaboration enhances our creative journey, as it provides fresh perspectives, new ideas, and a sense of accountability. When we collaborate, we learn from each other's approaches and find new ways to integrate our skills and talents into our creative process. Collaborative creativity fosters a sense of mutual support and growth, where we celebrate each other's contributions and find joy in the collective experience.

The spirit of collaboration is a reminder that creativity is not a solitary pursuit, but a shared journey filled with connection and growth. By embracing this spirit with bold strokes and gentle hands, we cultivate a sense of self-compassion and creativity that allows us to create and connect.

14

Chapter 14: The Gift of Gratitude

Gratitude is a powerful and transformative aspect of the creative process, allowing us to appreciate the beauty and joy of our creations and the journey that brought them to life. The gift of gratitude lies in its ability to connect us to our true selves and to the world around us, fostering a sense of fulfillment and purpose.

Self-compassion is essential in embracing the gift of gratitude, as it encourages us to be kind to ourselves and to appreciate our creative efforts. By being gentle with ourselves and acknowledging our need for gratitude, we create a space where appreciation can flourish. Self-compassion allows us to find joy in the process of creation and to celebrate our achievements.

Building together through gratitude enhances our creative journey, as collaboration provides support and encouragement. When we express gratitude together, we foster a sense of connection and collective growth. Collaborative gratitude encourages us to appreciate each other's contributions and to find joy in the shared experience.

The gift of gratitude is a reminder that creativity is not just about producing tangible results, but about experiencing the joy and fulfillment of the creative process. By embracing this gift with bold strokes and gentle hands, we cultivate a sense of self-compassion

continue

The gift of gratitude is a reminder that creativity is not just about producing tangible results, but about experiencing the joy and fulfillment of the creative process. By embracing this gift with bold strokes and gentle hands, we cultivate a sense of self-compassion and connection that enriches our lives and our creative journey.

15

Chapter 15: The Legacy of Creativity

Creativity leaves a lasting legacy, shaping the world and inspiring future generations. The legacy of creativity lies in its ability to transcend time and space, touching the hearts and minds of people across the globe. It is through our creative endeavors that we leave a mark on the world, sharing our unique perspectives and contributions.

Self-compassion is essential in embracing the legacy of creativity, as it encourages us to be kind to ourselves and to recognize the value of our creative efforts. By being gentle with ourselves and acknowledging our need for self-expression, we create a space where our legacy can flourish. Self-compassion allows us to celebrate our achievements and to find meaning in the impact of our creativity.

Building together with others enhances the legacy of creativity, as collaboration fosters a sense of collective growth and contribution. When we create together, we share our stories and experiences, building a tapestry of creativity that reflects our diverse perspectives and talents. Collaborative creativity encourages us to find strength in our collective contributions and to leave a lasting legacy that inspires future generations.

The legacy of creativity is a testament to the transformative power of the creative process. It is a reminder that our creativity can shape the world and touch the lives of others. By embracing this legacy with bold strokes and gentle hands, we cultivate a sense of self-compassion and creativity that allows us to create and connect.

16

Chapter 16: The Journey of Self-Discovery

Creativity is a journey of self-discovery, where we explore our inner selves and uncover new facets of our identity. The journey of self-discovery lies in its ability to connect us to our true selves, allowing us to express our thoughts, emotions, and experiences through our creative endeavors.

Self-compassion plays a key role in the journey of self-discovery, as it encourages us to be kind to ourselves and to embrace our creative process with curiosity and wonder. By being gentle with ourselves and acknowledging our need for self-exploration, we create a space where self-discovery can occur. Self-compassion allows us to find joy in the process of creation and to celebrate our unique perspectives.

Building together with others enhances our journey of self-discovery, as collaboration provides support, encouragement, and diverse perspectives. When we create together, we share our stories and experiences, fostering a sense of connection and collective growth. Collaborative creativity encourages us to learn from each other's journeys and to find inspiration in our shared experiences.

The journey of self-discovery is a reminder that creativity is not just about producing tangible results, but about exploring our inner selves and finding meaning in our experiences. By embracing this journey with bold strokes and gentle hands, we cultivate a sense of self-compassion and creativity that allows us to create and connect.

17

Chapter 17: The Art of Building Together

Building together is the culmination of creativity, self-compassion, and collaboration. The art of building together lies in its ability to foster a sense of connection and collective growth, where we celebrate each other's unique contributions and find joy in the shared experience.

Self-compassion is essential in the art of building together, as it encourages us to approach our collaborative efforts with kindness and respect. By being gentle with ourselves and acknowledging our need for mutual support, we create a space where collaboration can thrive. Self-compassion allows us to communicate openly, to listen actively, and to embrace the contributions of others.

Building together with others enhances our creative journey, as it provides fresh perspectives, new ideas, and a sense of accountability. When we collaborate, we learn from each other's approaches and find new ways to integrate our skills and talents into our creative process. Collaborative creativity fosters a sense of mutual support and growth, where we celebrate each other's contributions and find joy in the collective experience.

The art of building together is a reminder that creativity is not a solitary pursuit, but a shared journey filled with connection and growth. By embracing this art with bold strokes and gentle hands, we cultivate a sense of self-compassion and creativity that allows us to create and connect.

Bold Strokes, Gentle Hands: Creativity, Self-Compassion, and the Art of Building Together

Book Description:

In a world brimming with noise and haste, there lies an oasis where creativity, self-compassion, and collaboration flourish. "Bold Strokes, Gentle Hands" invites you on a transformative journey through the realms of imagination and self-discovery.

This book is an intimate exploration of the creative process, emphasizing the importance of approaching your endeavors with both bold strokes of courage and gentle hands of kindness. Whether you're an artist, writer, entrepreneur, or simply someone looking to infuse more creativity into your life, this book offers a profound and practical guide to navigating your creative journey.

Through seventeen thoughtfully crafted chapters, you will delve into the myriad facets of creativity. From embracing the blank canvas and the dance of ideas to the healing power of creativity and the magic of flow, each chapter offers insights, exercises, and reflections designed to nurture your creative spirit.

At the heart of this journey is the practice of self-compassion. You will learn to be kind to yourself, to view mistakes as opportunities for growth, and to find joy in the process rather than fixating on the outcome. Self-compassion becomes the bedrock upon which your creative endeavors stand, allowing you to explore, experiment, and express with authenticity and grace.

But creativity does not thrive in isolation. "Bold Strokes, Gentle Hands" also emphasizes the art of building together. Collaboration is celebrated as a powerful force that enriches our creative journeys, fosters mutual support, and amplifies our collective potential. By merging diverse perspectives and skills, we create something greater than the sum of its parts.

In this book, you will find a harmonious blend of inspiration and practicality, infused with warmth and wisdom. "Bold Strokes, Gentle Hands" is an invitation to embrace your creative potential, to cultivate self-compassion, and to build a world of beauty, connection, and fulfillment—one bold stroke and gentle hand at a time.

www.ingramcontent.com/pod-product-compliance
Lightning Source LLC
LaVergne TN
LVHW020500080526
838202LV00057B/6067